ALL PRAISE BELONGS TO GOD

Other Works by James A Stump

Walks Along the Pier:
Tales of a Wounded Healer
A novel about the counseling profession

Psychotherapy: All the Dirty Little Secrets Your
Therapist Doesn't Want You To Know
A guide to selecting your personal
psychotherapist!

Inspirational Stories:
Christmas Oranges
Douglas
Judah's Coming
The Seventh King

Christmas Threes
Three short vignettes for the stage:
The Christmas Thief
Christmas Neighbors
A Christmas Vignette

Counselor's Couch

ILSA

Fiction

By

JAMES A STUMP

Licensed Marriage & Family Therapist

ILSA

Of all the gin joints of all the towns in all the world…

she *had to walk into mine.*

      It was late afternoon – almost dinnertime - on an idyllic Southern California 'Endless Summer' type of day. When I agreed to the appointment on the phone (Don't ask me why: some unidentified pheromone in her voice, I suspect,) she instructed me to meet her at Austin's – an upscale restaurant that occupied the entire second level at the north end of the pier. Haughty, elegant, aloof – and expensive – Austin's detached itself from the plebeian areas of the pier and reigned over an exclusively beautiful vista of sparkling ocean and romantic sunsets.

I arrived on time to discover that Ilsa had not. Since I could not afford its prices and it was not my dime, I chose to loiter in the lobby area in front of the bar. The Austin dressed itself in windows – three hundred and sixty degree, floor to ceiling, tinted apertures that allowed patrons to peer out without allowing commoners to glimpse in. While I waited I took advantage of the rarely-before-seen-by-me panorama of sun, sand, surf and pier, and amused myself with my favorite pastime: people watching.

From the perch that the Austin provided, I could see the entire pier as it bowed out and away to the south and east. Every inch of decking from the entrance past the tourist shops and restaurants curving around the fishing areas and traveling straight at me to the door below my feet was engulfed in humanity. All types of people strolled the boardwalk from retired couples risking their lives against melanoma to middle class families attempting to enjoy fleeting days of togetherness to groups of working class types fishing for free dinners. Not to mention a few kids sucking on marijuana who gigglingly believed they had discovered the secrets of the universe. On that afternoon there were so many people passing in and out of the throng that it was easy to view them as a collective 'sea of humanity' and hard to distinguish any one as an individual.

Until Ilsa stepped onto my pier.

Ilsa resembled Alyssa - the tragic love-of-my-life - perfectly and because of that unfortunate resemblance she evoked pangs of regret so deep that I thought I would drown in my bitter memories.

When Ilsa climbed the stairs from the parking structure and stepped onto the boardwalk, I noticed her. She didn't exactly emit the same vibrational frequency that Alyssa did but they were quite similar. And because my radar had picked her out,I instantly performed a mental identification check. No – she wasn't my Alyssa – but she was of a kind.

I watched her – Ilsa, that is - and was amazed at the similarities. The same healthy, trim – yet curvaceous – body type. The same 'professional playing hooky' presentation and attire: loose white thigh-length shorts, hot pink top tied up under sumptuous breasts, matching pink visor stuffed into spills of flowing blond hair; golden necklace, golden bracelet, over-sized sunglasses all clinging to a luscious tan that spanned inviting arms and legs that shot forever down into beaded white Espadrille sandals. I just knew she wore a golden ankle bracelet – I just *knew* it.

As she strode onto the pier with her right hand clutching the long strap of an over-sized bag slung over a shoulder and her left hand clutching car keys – BMW, was my guess: no sense showing off – she glanced at her oversized wristwatch and frowned. She walked with confidence but also with purpose as if not wanting to slow down for fear of contracting some local malady. Her head turned left, then right, then back again; her lips parted slightly as if she were vulnerable, lost and needing direction. But I knew the purpose of her Alyssa-esque maneuvers: a turning head produced flouncing curls – the better to catch and reflect the light. And to attract the eyes of inferior males – several of which, I could see from my observatory, spoke to her – presumably asking if she required assistance in locating anything – a restaurant, a bar or, perhaps, a *date*? The fingers of her left hand splayed out against them - no, thanks – but, oh, so slender and deliciously tipped in sharp designer nails that begged to scratch and slice and...

But I digress.

Ilsa bobbed her way up the main thorough-fare, never stopping but having to say 'no, thank you' several times before reaching the sport fishing deck. There she spun on the delicate toes of her elegant sandals before retreating the way she had come. At the junction, she scanned the boardwalk in front of the restaurants and the open air concessions before pirouetting left and executing a second run along the crowded – but smaller and therefore less populated – transect of the pier.

Again, the male eyes and invitations; again the vulnerable dismissals. Having reconnoitered the main bodies of the pier, and with a final fling of her head in curl tousling expertise, Ilsa made straight for the front door of Austin's – clearly having known where it stood from the beginning of her exhibition. As I watched her enter from my elevated perspective, I smiled to myself and silently applauded her brilliant performance: she had turned every male head worth turning in an ego-reassuring tour de triumph of the entire pier.

I turned toward the stairwell and awaited her arrival like an attentive house servant. As she ascended she slipped into a light white jacket which dressed her up nicely for the restaurant; the lady certainly had her fashion sense. She entered like a queen and, pretending not to notice me, she spoke to the maître d'. "I have a reservation. Ilsa?"

"Of course. Right this way."

She sallied off leaving me to figure out how to enter the presence.

I followed along, allowed the maître d' to seat her, and then introduced myself. "Excuse me. Are you Ilsa? You asked me to meet you here?"

"Doug?"

"Yes," I said, so proud of her success.

"Please," she said waving at the chair opposite hers. "Join me."

I maneuvered around the waiter – who eyed my Men's House gabardine slacks doubtfully – and took a seat, saying, "So... What can I do for you?"

Ever so slightly Ilsa's head tilted back and away from my words. Then she flashed an indulgent smile at me as if, even though I had committed the worst kind of social gaffe, she intended to magnanimously overlook it. She said,

"Let's order first. Dinner is on me. Anything you'd like."

A waiter set a menu across my plate that I dutifully opened and scanned. The prices caught in my throat and I said, "I'll have coffee and a garden salad."

"Nonsense," Ilsa stated. "I promised you a meal!" Looking coquettishly up at the waiter, she said, "I've decided on the specialty of the house. We'll have the Quiche Austin, sliced tomatoes with vinaigrette. I know it's a bit early for red but since it accentuates so well, a bottle of Cabernet – the Mondovi, I think. Croissant, please, with honeyed butter and sparkling water."

It was in no way my idea of 'a meal.' In order to head off what would be for me an indigestible agony, I almost whispered, "I'm sorry but I don't eat quiche, I don't drink alcohol and," just to even the score on some of what I owed her psychological equivalent, "I'm not fond of vinaigrette."

"You'll eat this," she assured me. She handed the waiter her menu and off he went dooming me to an unpalatable gustatory future.

I had no idea how to respond to that treatment – after all, she was buying - so I tried to ignore it and focus on my hostess. Clearly she was used to being in charge – apparently of *everything* in the lives of those around her. I felt unacknowledged and dismissed and imagined that all of her associates and coworkers – perhaps everyone in her life - felt the same. Was *that* why she had called me? Relationship conflicts?

"I imagine you're wondering why I called you."

Okay. Either she was a mind reader or she had heard me when I asked that question the *first* time.

"My doctor says I have high blood pressure."

"Sorry to hear that."

"She says I need to relax – reduce my level of stress."

"Sounds like good advice."

Ilsa shot an evil look at me. "Are you trying to be *flip*pant?"

I inexplicably felt defensive and realized that was her intent – consciously or unconsciously. Waiting silently – and giving her time to reconsider her deportment - I 'breathed' her in, being careful not to look directly into her eyes, for if I had, she would have read the gist of what I was thinking and feeling.

I stared at the white linen covering the table until I identified my feelings and from where they had come.

Alyssa.

Alyssa had used similarly dismissive behavior long ago. The words were slightly different but the intention was the same: intimidation. Then, as now, I had uttered absolutely nothing in word or insinuation that was meant to be disagreeable. I tried to consider what that indicated therapeutically but my analytical skill eluded me. I was too caught up in my negative emotional deja vu.

I looked across the table and realized that for Ilsa *this* was her best behavior – but it wasn't going to last for long.

So, apologetically I said, "Please, let me start over. How can I help?" knowing all too well that I was *not going* to help, not while I remained immersed in feelings of countertransference from a former lover.

"I've tried yoga, Tai Chi, kick boxing, running, meditation, weight training, diet, smiling, positive thinking and every other damn thing anyone could think of. Now I'm going to try counseling," she told me.

You are? "And what would be your purpose in that?"

She glared at me as if - at that moment - I were the imbecile I felt I was. (She just *brought out* the defiance in me!) "To reduce my blood pressure!"

Of course. Foolish of me to ask. "There are any number of counselors in the area. Why come to me?"

She smiled the kind of smile that told me she was going to lie. "I heard you were kind of quirky. I like that kind of thing."

Right. A 'new adventure' – one she could tell all her friends about – the quirky therapist who simply was not smart enough to outsmart Ilsa. Maybe by meeting me she had changed her mind. Not about the 'smart' part but about 'liking that kind of thing.'

"Tell me about yourself."

"Is this where we get all psychoanalytical?"

I shrugged my shoulders in an attempt to hide my irritation. I wanted to say, '*You* called *me*! What the hell do you want?' but I was aware that the irritation was mine, not hers, even though she was passive-aggressively inciting that irritation. I stifled my as yet unspoken retort and said instead, "If I'm going to be able to do anything for you, I will need to know something about you."

With faux exuberance, she said, "You want personal history. Right!" She then chanted out the following: "Let's see, if you're Family Systems, you'll want to know about my parents, grandparents, siblings and even the dog. If you're Object Relations, it's just my mother. Cognitive Behavioral, you'll challenge my irrational beliefs. Transactional, we're both okay. Rogerian, you'll tell me I'm great no matter what I say. I won't go to group therapy. NLP, you'll match my kinesthesia…Ooo! If you try Gestalt on me, I'll bat you with a rolled up copy of *Elle* but I'd *love* to tell you my dreams, Doctor Jung! You choose."

I laughed in spite of myself. If Ilsa was not a therapist in hiding, she was certainly an over-achiever. And obviously highly intelligent. She wouldn't attend group counseling – which suggested she was hiding emotional pain and lacked trust. Antisocial? Somewhat. I had a hunch that she didn't truly feel anything so she was lying to herself about the kinesthesia. I couldn't imagine working for this woman – unless I was the type who thrived on abusive micromanagement. Her manner of dress told me she was concerned about 'appearances' and her behavior while transecting the pier indicated that she enjoyed the attention of men but didn't really want to know one. I guessed that she was promiscuous in a 'use and discard anonymously' pattern, not wanting to face the evidence of her human need. She would *never* tell me her dreams – not her real ones. And no amount of unconditional positive regard would ever convince her she was 'okay' because all of her behavior was driven by the proverbial underlying sense of inferiority. Which was why she was a work-a-holic and had high blood pressure.

All of this too familiar.

And largely unworkable. That is, my specu-lation was that she wouldn't *want* therapy to succeed because she wouldn't want to honestly face any of her emotional issues. She struck me as a woman who would cling to her dysfunction as if it were a matter of life or death. Which it was –

emotionally – for her. If a counselor *could* some-how convince her to drop her defenses without her desire for change, she would implode; disappear into an emotional black hole. And that was some-thing she simply would *not* allow.

But something more than that was wrong – obviously. People like Ilsa didn't even consider counseling unless they were in some kind of trouble – some kind of pain that they couldn't handle on their own. A pain she had not yet identified. *My* question was: how to help her identify it?

Stress. She said her problem was high blood pressure – which likely meant stress. I was sure she pushed herself harder than was necessary but I could also imagine that her occupation came with *necessary* stressors.

What to do?

Back to basics. Form a relationship. Decide if I could – or even *wanted* – to help her. Determine if *she* actually wanted any help.

"What kind of work do you do?"

"Own my own company – advertising. I occupy the top floor of the Strathmore Hotel here on the beach – small but it has history. I could have gone downtown but traffic is such a bore. Besides – my clients can come to *me*."

'Own.' Not 'run' or 'operate' – *'own'*. She made sure to mention that first. And the Strathmore was three stories high and a block wide – right on the Strand facing the ocean. A pinch of grandiosity there – probably necessary to cap the negative introjects in the Id. "I assume you have employees?"

"Six. Mostly graphic artists for layout design. I do the rest."

"No office manager or financial partner? No sales personnel?"

She glared at me: how could I have been so impudent? "No. *I* do all that."

"What would your life be like if you didn't own your own business?"

"What is this? An illogical intersession?"

I assumed she was referring to 'paradoxical intervention'. Or maybe she meant 'paradoxical directive' but neither idea was an appropriate response to my question. Perhaps she had intended it as a bit of humor: an intentional mis-statement to demonstrate her superior knowledge. Regardless of any of that, I didn't correct her; I *did* allow myself a nanosecond of superiority – on the off chance that she actually *had* made a mistake. But her aggressive manner had me feeling defensive again; so I chose my words very carefully. "No. I'm just asking. I would imagine that your responsibilities are contributing to your stress and I wondered what your life would be like without as much responsibility."

The waiter arrived to show Ilsa the label on the wine she had ordered. After she had glanced at it and nodded, he deftly removed the cork and set it within her easy reach. Ilsa absently picked it up and felt its aquosity to assure herself that the wine had been stored properly on its side while the waiter poured a sample for her. She had been giving me an 'evil eye' but broke off for a moment to inspect, swirl, breathe and taste her sample. Finally she gave her approval and when the waiter hurried off to decant the wine, she said, "Never happen. That company is *mine* and I won't give it up. Next question."

This lady would be a hard nut to crack. Especially if she didn't want to be cracked. But without some connection, some agreed purpose to our conversation, we would accomplish nothing and either she would walk away convinced that therapists were worthless or I would have to decline working with her. Which for that moment I didn't want to do.

Which, for me, was a curious thing.

I decided that either way I had nothing to lose so I 'went for it.'

"What drives you?"

An eyebrow jumped up on her perfect forehead. Had I offended her? Again? How? By coming too close to that problem that she had even yet not identified?

"Making something of my life. Success. Being in charge. The usual things."

The usual things – for men. All the goals she had cited were traditionally male ambitions. She may as well have included power – and the abusive use of it.

"I'm in charge of my own destiny, my own life," she said. "Nobody controls me."

Of course not: you control them. And I had noticed that she had offered that information. I hadn't asked for it. How and why had this woman gotten under my skin? And so quickly. "Is it lonely?"

For the first time since I met her, she displayed a hint of feeling, some vulnerability that suggested humanness: she dropped her gaze, her look softened. But she quickly buried this truth by retaking control of her expression and issuing an evasive command. "I have 'friends.' Eat your salad."

Do you? Have friends? I wondered. Other than sex partners? I said, "Tell me about your 'friends.'" I realized I was taking chances – questioning her statement and issuing an order. Controlling personalities love to *give* orders but refuse to *take* them. And they *hate* to be questioned.

"Why do you want to know about *them*?"

Of course. This was all about *Ilsa*, not her *friends*. Narcissistic features? She was too smart to be fooled by popular therapeutic techniques, tricks and gimmicks. So I decided to use the oldest trick of all: the truth. Only - therapists call this 'transparency' by which they mean they tell the client what they are doing and invite the client to participate in the process of exploring issues. It's supposed to give the client a sense of empowerment through joining with the counselor for a common goal. Sometimes it even works.

"The truth is, I want to know about *you*. But so far you haven't told me anything of a personal nature. I thought it might be easier for you to talk about some of the peripheral aspects of your life and in that way I might get to know you in an oblique manner."

"I've told you a lot about myself."

Other times it doesn't work. Transparency, that is.

"You've named your profession and your professional goals and told me that you have 'friends' but you really haven't confided anything about yourself. Nothing personal."

"I'm not here to talk about anything personal. I'm here to talk about stress."

"So, are we agreeing that the problem is stress caused by...?"

"The problem is high blood pressure which *you* are doing nothing to lower. What do you think you're up to?"

"I'm trying to figure out how counseling can help you. You said you called because of high blood pressure. You said you've been to a doctor and presumably you've explored medications but you're still seeking help. You said you tried many physical activities to reduce your high blood pressure. You obviously know a great deal about therapy, so either you've been through a lot of counseling or you've read prodigiously. Maybe both. So what's going to be different this time? How can I help?"

Ilsa hesitated, glared, gulped some wine and then began to speak. When she did, it was more like counseling was expected to be. But she did it with resentment.

"You want me to say that I had terrible parents," she said.

No, I didn't! Why did she bring *that* up? Was that *her* idea of therapy? "Did you?"

"No! My father was kind, just disappointed."

"What do you mean?"

"He wanted a son. He loved me...but he wanted a son."

"And your mother?"

"My mother was disappointed also...in my father. I think she felt she had married beneath her."

"How so?"

"Mother was beautiful. She could have married anybody she wanted. Dad…was just a great guy."

"Do you have brothers or sisters?"

"No."

"Did you want them?"

"No."

"How did your parents get along?"

"Normal, I guess. I remember when I was really young they used to argue a lot and then they just stopped. From then on the house was peaceful."

Peaceful. I could imagine that her parents didn't 'stop' arguing: they *gave up* arguing. Maybe they gave up on their marriage as well and resigned themselves to lives of quiet desperation. From that point on their resignation was the elephant in the home that no one ever talked about. If so, had it played itself out in a loveless marriage that radiated no emotional warmth for the daughter? And given the absence of actual unconditional positive regard, had Ilsa directed her energy toward education, success, accomplishments? Had she become successful at success? In order to gain her parents' approval? Attention? Notice? *Any*thing?

Those were my unconfirmed guesses.

But at least Ilsa was talking and I didn't want her to stop.

"Start at the beginning. Tell me about your parents – where they came from, how they met, occupations. Then tell me what it was like for you to grow up in their home, what your life was like."

With a sigh that felt like her parents' resignation, Ilsa began. And the story she told was one that I could have told for her. It was that déjà vu all over again. But she did what I asked her to do: she talked. And while she talked, I studied her. But not with my customarily clinical detachment.

I was thinking about – and remembering – Alyssa. And I knew it.

I have always had a kind of radar where Alyssa was concerned. If I entered a room full of people, I knew instantly if she was there; even when I couldn't see her, I could sense her presence. If a phone rang, I could feel whether or not it was her calling. Driving on a street, I could detect if she were in the area. Mind you, I could never figure out anything else about her – what she was thinking, what she was feeling, what she wanted. Or what she needed. But *where* she *was* – that came to me as readily as a heartbeat. It was as if she sent out radio signals that I was attuned to.

I gazed across the elegantly set table at Austin's and marveled at the similarities between Ilsa and my Alyssa.

I guessed Ilsa's height at about five foot four – just like Alyssa. Her age, about thirty-four, which was Alyssa's age the last time I saw her. Ilsa was curvaceous – in the way I like women to be. Just like Alyssa. Voluptuous hips I would have liked to hold, breasts I would have gone to jail to get lost in. Eyes that bore down as she pronounced her 'serious' points. Cheeks I could have gently kissed; lips I would have taken by force. A neck I might have intertwined with mine certain that the touch of her skin was soft, feminine, inviting. I didn't have to imagine making love to her: I *knew* what that would be like. Legs intertwined; bodies fitting perfectly. A slight gasp, a moan, and I would feel powerful, masculine, immortal – until that little death, that wave of ocean pounding the shore, spending itself in a rush that would eventually disappear into – her.

Ilsa talked and I pretended to be paying attention. But I wasn't. Not at all. I was lost in my ongoing struggle with the memory of Alyssa.

Why had I wanted to succeed in a relationship with a woman who clearly did not have the attraction for me that I had for her? She could behave as badly as she pleased because she wasn't concerned about our success or failure. To her, it didn't seem to matter. *My* need must have come from my own failed dreams and desires. But why did Alyssa remain in our relationship as long as she did? I suspect it was because I allowed her to project her unresolved conflicts onto me. But I never found out because she never shared any of her feelings with me. Except her anger, of course. *That* she let me have regularly.

And I had a suspicion that Ilsa was a similar type of woman. She appeared to want to keep me feeling off balance and insecure. Maybe that's what triggered my unfortunate emotional response to her.

While Ilsa continued to talk, I tried to sort all of that out.

I often thought that Alyssa had been trying to chase me away, to push me out of her life because she didn't have the courage to end our relationship directly; she didn't want to have to be the one who ended it. So she treated me badly in the hope that *I* would be the one to 'go away.' And eventually I had to do just that. When I no longer could stand the pain of her rejection. What hurt the most was that I was unable to conquer her demons and win her affection. I thought that 'love would find a way' to overcome everything.

That was the supreme ignorance of my life. And she was my sublime failure. Whatever her reasons for her behavior, I was never to know. But the awareness of her objective did come to strike me like a thunderbolt one night when I was walking over a bridge.

Alyssa – the memories, the sensations, the scent…

Scent!

I looked over at Ilsa and surreptitiously inhaled. I didn't know what perfume she was wearing but it was the same fragrance that Alyssa used to wear. I should have noticed it earlier. Olfactory stimulation can be a strong trigger of memory. Alyssa refused to tell me the name of her perfume because she said she never wanted me to give it to anyone else.

That had been her kindest moment, the only indication that she had had any positive affection for me at all. Out of homage to the feelings I still held for Alyssa, I would not ask Ilsa for the name. The scent was hypnotic, exotic and – I was certain – expensive. I left the secret with Alyssa but I was helpless to escape the torrential memories it recalled in me.

I first laid eyes on Alyssa at a book convention. I was there with a psychology professor of mine to observe rapacious human behavior; Alyssa was there to promote her company. Even before we met I knew we weren't 'right' for each other. She was beautiful, glamorous (not the same thing) abundantly intelligent; a Type 1A overachiever on a fast track to financial independence. I enjoyed sunsets, water colors and intellectual discussion. She described herself as 'pragmatic'; 'unemotional' - in what later proved to be 'unavailable'. I wore my heart on my sleeve – not as a rule, only for her. She tore them both off – the heart *and* the sleeve - threw them away; said they were impractical. That was her way of showing concern for my wellbeing.

With Alyssa I became less assertive; to which she became more aggressive, then domineering all the way to punishing. She told me she had no need for lies, that she was honest at all times. But 'truth' became her weapon until it finally gave way to untruth. Perhaps the only *other* indication of humanness she ever offered me, the only other hint of emotional attachment: she was unable to end our relationship. So, lies. Lies she wanted me to discover so that *I* would leave the relationship.

She told me she was strong – also not true. She was defended; she would not reveal her vulnerability to anyone. The only problem with that was that it kept her locked away – from me, from life, from herself. But I understood: she was defending herself against feeling her feelings for fear she would have to feel them. *Because* my continued presence in her life would have forced her to admit some sort of 'imperfection' – that she had a human need for relationship - I finally had to accept the fact that we wouldn't be successful as a couple – no matter how hard I tried to accommodate her emotional needs. I knew I was obstructing her freedom to seek someone who was...who would... I can't bring myself to think it. Even now.

But the questions that had continued to haunt me were: why was I so helplessly attracted to someone who was obviously not a good match for me? And: what sort of imprinting had such a hold on me that I would continue to cling to such an unfulfilling memory? They were the sorts of questions I used to ask my clients to answer so that they might overcome their neurotic compulsions and create happier futures.

In the end, I could only come to two conclusions:

We all have our 'Fatal Attractions.'

And...

Alyssa is mine.

Austin waiters came and went. Food was placed on the table. One waiter's culinary attentions nudged my attention back into the moment. And back onto Ilsa's 'story.'

When I 'mentally checked in' to learn what Ilsa was talking about, I found her engaged in a presentation of her childhood years, berating me for not understanding what was obviously the problem: she was too special for her beginnings. She had wanted better schools, wealthier neighborhoods, unlimited access to the finer possibilities of life. Her parents *would* have provided same but circumstances beyond their control prevented it.

"I argued with my parents – like all adolescents will do. But I eventually won – of course. And what I won was the 'right' to make my own decisions. I'm sure you'll agree that individuation is a normal process of growth for teenagers. But I was all of *sixteen* at the time!"

Such a superior person, I thought cynically. But my cynicism didn't interrupt the flow of her heroic autobiography.

"I enrolled early in a not-so-prestigious college, then a better graduate school – not what I would have liked..."

...or what she felt she deserved...

"...but serviceable. It was no matter. I parlayed my 'native abilities', shall we say, into a 'presence' in the business community and made my own success. Since then, I have traveled to all the places that I should have visited when I was younger..."

...the experiences that she felt were her birthright but that her parents failed to provide...

"...and made my own way in life."

...which was why she had set her sights on personal excellence.

She absentmindedly chewed a bit of tomato and ruminated, "My parents and I are close but I don't get to see them very often, I'm so busy and all."

But they understood and were very proud of her, she told me. She had a minor concern about her mother's depression but it was really no problem at all.

Just like Alyssa. Who might have said all that and more.

My lord, what had I fallen into?

I was mixing and confusing my client with my one significant relationship – my *failed* relationship, at that - and such emotional confusion wasn't good for any of us.

Purposefully and professionally I tried to set aside my memories and focus on the woman across the table from me – the attractive, affluent one who was droning on about the slights life had dealt her. And although I struggled virtuously, professionalism eluded me: she was so much like my Alyssa.

"My parents weren't – and *aren't*," Ilsa assured me, "bad people. But they were – and *are* – limited. They gave what they had to give. I…had to make my way almost entirely on my own."

Such a brave girl. And so selfless, I thought sarcastically. There she was, superior to her parents in every way but with never a word of reprobation. Unless one considered the numerous implications of parental failure and life's unjustified lack of appreciation for such obviously meritorious personal attributes as those possessed by the self-deprecating Ilsa.

See? I can talk good too.

I didn't wonder that my attention had wandered. Egotism can be so boring – just by sitting at the table. But I did wonder if this particular egotism had spilled into narcissism which I didn't care to work with. I didn't suspect that Ilsa was the latter but I wasn't certain I wanted to deal with her if she was the former.

I looked across the table and assessed my challenge. What would Alyssa have done if confronted with Ilsa? She would have smiled agreeably then quickly excused herself. Two queens cannot exist in the same vacuum: not enough oxygen for either one; not enough spotlight; not enough attention. But I wasn't Alyssa. So like the fool I am and always will be, I sallied forth on my quixotic adventure, doomed from the very start but unable to stop myself. Like the proverbial moth, I was drawn to the flame; had to immolate myself on the altar of impossible relationships. That's counter-transference at work.

Ilsa was saying...

"So I simply presented myself at the dean's door and insisted on an interview." Two beats in order that I might appreciate the significance of a fearless nineteen-year-old challenging the established order of a renowned university. "She saw me. And once I was in the door, I *knew* the scholarship was mine. That was the second one, of course. After that, they all knew who I was and I was unofficially invited into the club."

The 'club of overly-achieving graduate students', in case I was wondering.

At some point I was required to assert my therapeutic presence – or at least to make it known. If I hadn't I would have relegated myself to the role of doting admirer. But that's not how change occurs. Or how counseling succeeds. Or for that matter how blood pressure is lowered. "You've been through a lot," I observed. "You've had many good experiences."

"I've earned them all," she corrected me.

"Of course," I admitted, humbly chastising myself for a verbally clumsy lout. "Still – all of it must have taken its toll."

Ilsa glared at me as if I was a larva in her Vinaigrette. "I *handled* it," she said more as a threat than as an item of information. "But that was *nothing* compared to the challenges of opening an ad agency.

"After my Fillmore Scholarship, I had my pick of any number of positions in New York. But, of course, I had to be on my own. And I thought – 'mom and dad are getting older' so I really *should* locate on the west coast. So I packed up my Fellowships and my award-winning portfolio and I..."

I knew if I didn't interrupt her self-centered recitation and convince her to focus on the problem at hand, my presence was pointless and when she eventually grew tired of entertaining me with narratives of her greatness, she would dismiss me. But breaking into her verbal cyclo-rama would be difficult. Ilsa would view any interruption as an insult.

When she paused for a lubricative sip of cabernet, I ventured forth.

"You've accomplished much," I reiterated. "And I can appreciate what it took to do all that. And how it might have resulted in your current stress. What do you suppose therapy could do to help you with that?"

Ilsa blinked, resettled her offended ego – I *had* interrupted her, hadn't I? - then launched forward in a new direction – one of *her* choosing, of course. "Why, now that I think of it, *nothing*," she said with a little smile. "There is nothing you can do for me. I realized on my way up here that I was just being silly. A momentary lapse, a passing mood. I took care of it."

Her reaction was exactly what I didn't want – yet exactly what I expected. I had to coax her toward a mutual interaction or surrender the challenge. "What did you take care of?"

Another interruption equaled insult equaled glare. "I beg your pardon?"

"You said you 'took care' of something. What did you take care of?"

Ilsa blinked uncomprehendingly. But something had reached her – perhaps something underneath her conscious awareness – and below her emotional defenses. She considered the question, apparently couldn't think of a cover-up fast enough and attempted to conceal the real issue – whatever that was - by stalling for time. "I don't know what you mean."

In order to help the process along (the process of identifying subconscious motivation), I made a few suggestions. "When you were coming onto the pier, were you annoyed with someone?"

There was a beat before she said, "I don't know *what* I was. It's not relevant."

I was certain a Fillmore Scholar had a better memory than that. "Were you feeling rushed because you were late?"

Ilsa smiled her brightest and most disingenuous smile; her eyes virtually danced in their own light as, up and down, she batted her brushed-on lashes. "I'm always late and I never feel rushed. Nothing's so important it can't wait."

She meant that I and everybody else in her life were unimportant so *we* can wait. "What irritated you?"

More bats of the imperial lashes. "*Nothing.*"

"Then why did you have to 'take care of it'?"

Ilsa picked up her wine glass, placed her elbows on the table and created a shield by rolling the glass between both palms. "Boy," she said. "You're like a pit bull. Do you sink your teeth into all your little patients?"

Given that Ilsa had dominated the previous half-hour with self-congratulatory hot air, I understood that her last comments were both a 'meant to be insulting' assessment of me and a warning to back off. I knew I couldn't engage defensively in any of her challenges or the game was lost. "I'm wondering what you were 'being silly' about," I said. (Okay, okay. I was a little miffed. I'll admit it.)

Ilsa's smile went cold, flat − like a billboard ad for a soft drink that pretended to be happy but was devoid of 'fizz'. "*You* are becoming an*noy*ing," she told me.

Yes. When I'm good at my job. "Something had affected you in a negative manner," I said. "What was it?"

Ilsa sat – frozen in time. Then slowly arched an eyebrow as the corner of her mouth curled in on itself. Clearly she did not approve of being questioned about her dismissive behavior – even if obliquely. Since she looked like she might boil over at any second, I tried to calm her down by engaging her in some actual 'therapy'.

"You've tried everything else," I reminded her. "Yoga, Tai Chi, kick boxing, running, meditation, weight training, diet, positive thinking and every other damn thing anyone could think of. Now you said you were 'going to try' counseling. So...*try* it."

Fillmores aren't the only ones with good memory skills. While mental recall isn't my strongest suit, I have discovered that I have a facility for remembering what clients tell me. Human nature fascinates me.

"You forgot 'smiling'" she said.

"No, actually, I didn't. But since you have been smiling at me since we met, I assumed you hadn't yet discarded the technique along with all the others."

She took a beat or two; I could feel the computer computing behind the cute little squint in her eye. Then she smiled a genuine smile – likely the first real smile of her day – a decision had been made. "You are impudent. You know that, of course."

Popping a small black, pitted olive into my mouth – like Sylvester would pop Tweety – I answered, "Only when I'm working."

At that, she laughed a genuine laugh and I thought I had finally made a connection with the person behind the painted mask. "So, tell me, what annoys you?"

Ilsa dropped her shield, picked up a fork and twirled a bit of tomato in her Vinaigrette. "Lots of things. People, mostly."

I sipped sparkling water from a cut crystal goblet and 'interpreted' for her. "People just can't keep up with you?"

"No, it's not that. If somebody asks for help or information, I'm happy to give it. I take satisfaction from helping people."

And feeling superior to them, I thought - and realized my misdirected countertransference had popped up again. "What is it, then?" I asked to clarify her clarification and to keep myself focused. "What annoys you?"

"It's…when people don't *listen* to me."

Interesting. Although the lady presented as a woman who issued orders all day long, she didn't feel like anyone was listening to her. Could it be that the lady didn't feel *heard* – which most likely started in childhood? In her parents' emotional cold-storage domicile? Was *that* when she began her pursuit of perfection? Was that why she needed to be in charge? To be in 'control'? At that moment, it was just an assumption; a guess on my part. It would have to be checked and then explored; the hypothesis would need to be refined. "How do you handle it when people don't listen? How does it make you feel?"

"It makes me feel like nobody notices me," she said. "Like I don't matter. But when *I'm* running the place – they *listen*! They *have* to."

So she had to keep stacking up accomplishments in order to feel noticed, which was the only thing that made her feel alive. Classic issues. Classic reactive behavior. That's how we get all of our type 1 A work-a-holics. Success is great. Success is good. Unless it's being used to cover up feelings of low self-esteem. People who are 'driven' are not happy. And they act out their unhappiness in many – often hidden – ways.

I might have 'explored' Ilsa's feelings of 'I don't matter' and 'nobody notices me'. Stirring up her negative feelings would have been a good way of 'hooking' her into long-term therapy. But we were sitting in a busy, high-classed restaurant – not a good place for such a conversation if it were successful and Ilsa accessed some real feelings. And: by then I knew I was not going to work with her. She brought up too many countertransference feelings for me to ethically accept her as a client. I had decided that my goals for that meeting were to help her identify what was bothering her, point her in some direction that might be helpful and to suggest other professionals she might want to work on her issues with.

So I set my sights on issues that were hopefully not as deep as 'I don't matter' and said, "When you get a feeling like 'people aren't listening to me', what goes on in you? How do you respond?"

"I don't know what you mean."

"I mean, do you get angry? Do you snap at them? Do you raise your voice? Intimidate them? Or do you close down? Shut them out? Walk away or calmly tell them how you feel?" I knew which behavior I thought she employed; I was merely attempting to help her discover it for herself.

Ilsa shrugged her pretty shoulders. "I don't do any of that. I just get over it. After all, people who can't handle the truth aren't going to listen."

Interesting.

If I was going to believe her self-analysis – which I didn't – I would have had to believe that she used her will-power to overcome negative feelings then moved on without confronting the offender. *My* impression was that first she suppressed her feelings – stuffed them – then she dismissed the person who didn't do what she told them to do. (Even though *she* would never have complied if *they* had told *her* what to do.) Then - I suspected - her quickly-following next step would have been to get even. After all, what right did inferior people have to disrespect Ilsa? Not that I was judging her, of course. I was merely attempting to understand her emotional dilemma diagnostically. (Okay, okay. So I was lying to myself! I'll work on my own issues later.)

And I thought that underneath all that, what she was *really* doing was the exact opposite of what she *said* she was doing. I guessed that she *didn't* 'get over it': she got even. And that she 'couldn't handle the truth' so she rarely listened to it.

And she probably didn't know she was doing any of that.

In my imagination I could see Ilsa issuing orders to underlings who – in her opinion – had 'screwed up' by not listening to her.

That's what Alyssa would have done. She, also, had 'a need to be heard.'

Alyssa and I had had many hurtful exchanges. I was aware that I wasn't the cause of her unhappiness; I was just a 'punching bag', a means for her to discharge feelings that had been generated earlier in her life by some other 'failure to be heard'.

But even though I wasn't the 'cause', I wasn't the 'solution', either. I wasn't the one who could hold her and drain away all her pain with a hug. Alyssa wouldn't have allowed that: she would have thought of it as 'weakness'.

I did everything I could think of to support her but the more I allowed her to abuse me, the more she did abuse. Until I felt that *I* wasn't being heard. That's when I realized – one night on a bridge – that nothing was going to change. And that we were not going to be together.

I looked across the table at Ilsa.

She, too, was emotionally defended – with no way to acknowledge it. She used aggressiveness to protect herself because she, too, could not allow weakness. But pain bled through in other ways - like in abusive behavior toward a man who loved you - or perhaps something even simpler – like high blood pressure due to self-inflected stress.

No, I was not the right counselor for Ilsa. I mean, I could have sought out my own counseling to work on my feelings of hurt and rejection, my sense of loss and its unexpressed grief, to understand my obsessive attraction to an emotionally unavailable female. If I had done so, I might have been a better therapist, perhaps even a happier person. But that wasn't going to happen: I wasn't ready to give up Alyssa. Even if only the memory of her.

"Ilsa, you said you 'just got over it' when I asked you how you deal with feeling like people aren't listening to you. Could you describe that a little more?"

Ilsa shrugged. "I just let it go. I believe people have control over their bodies. The mind is part of the body. Therefore, people should be able to control their minds – control what they think. When I want to let go of something, I just put it out of my mind and focus on something else. It's simple."

"Are you able to let go of stress in the same way?"

Ilsa smiled: caught. "I would say 'yes' but obviously I haven't been completely successful as yet."

I smiled back at her: yep, I understand; and don't worry – that was just between us – now that we're friends.

"Tell me about your relationships."

I was changing up – going in another direction to circle around and come back at the same problem – stress – from a different angle. All roads lead to Rome. If Ilsa would talk about her personal relationships – which I suspected were many, superficial and all failed – I might identify a pattern of behavior for her. A pattern that might exonerate my poor work with her and that she could explore in her future therapy.

"Oooo! The sexy details!" she said. "Now we're going all Freudian. Which juicy morsel do you want? The first, the last or the best one who slipped in between?"

I let the innuendo slide – Freudian though it may have been. "I'll settle for a general overview. Are you in a relationship now?"

"No," she answered a bit too quickly. Had she recently condemned her latest admirer to her emotional guillotine? Or was she trying to convince herself that she had? Perhaps *she* was thinking the relationship had ended but the poor boy hadn't been notified as yet. Maybe she was in that stone-walling period in which she was ignoring him until he either went away or rekindled her interest.

"When was the last time you were in a relationship?"

"A while ago," she answered evasively.

What did that mean? "Last year? Last month? Last week?" I asked her. Yesterday…? I had to bite my tongue – *hard* – to resist saying, 'Last night?'

Ilsa thought it over; then decided to employ her smile therapy. "Recently," was all she would admit to me. "I haven't seen him in a few weeks."

"Why not?"

"We weren't getting along."

"How were you 'not getting along'?"

She flashed me her now-familiar glare of 'I hate being questioned' and said, "He's like all men. Possessive, controlling, wanting to run my life. You guys should know by now that I won't stand for it."

I let her use of the inclusive second person familiar slide by the boards and assessed the information she had – perhaps unintentionally – exposed. She had used the present tense. Did that suggest – as I suspected - that her latest battle-of-the-sexes wasn't quite over yet? The description she gave might as easily have described herself: did she reject that which she was? And she had used the words 'all men' to express an attitude of generalized rejection. Did that mean she had preempted even the possibility of relationship? Nothing new in any of that. But it *did* support some of my suspicions.

"What would you like in a relationship?"

"Someone who will *listen* to me! And understand what I'm saying."

Translation a la Alyssa: 'I want a man who will not challenge me, who will let me beat him up emotionally, who I can disrespect and eventually dump easily'. "That doesn't sound very difficult."

"Well, it seems to be. What is it with men?"

"What do you mean?"

"Why do men all have to be 'in charge' of everything? Why can't men have an equal relationship with a strong woman?"

I might have 'observed' that what most people – men *and* women – think of as 'strong' is usually 'abusive'. But I let that go as I knew it would be heard as contentious and not lead to anyplace productive. I also might have observed that millions of men and women have good – if not wonderful – relationships by being 'partners' – which is what I interpreted the word 'equal' to mean. But I let that idea go as well because I was fairly certain Ilsa didn't want anything near 'equality.'

"It sounds like that has been your experience in relationships - that men want to 'control' you."

"That and more," she said. "Men want to possess everything about me. Especially the way I think."

There was another 'issue' in that comment somewhere – one that I hoped we could identify. Something about 'thinking' – which I interpreted to be more about 'attitude' than a capacity of the mind. I let us both sit in that feeling for a long moment. Then I said, "It doesn't sound like any kind of relationship I'd want to be in."

"No," she agreed quietly.

I knew that Ilsa had contributed to her relationship problems. Just as I had contributed to mine and Alyssa had contributed to hers. But Ilsa's manner convinced me that she would not be able to 'hear' that about herself. She was nowhere near ready. She would likely take it as an insult and reject the insulter as just another person who 'doesn't listen to me'. And he was a man, to boot.

I assumed that Ilsa contributed to her relationship problems by (consciously or unconsciously) selecting unsuitable partners in order to support and reinforce her resentment against men. And that if she accidentally became involved in a potentially healthy relationship, she would sabotage it with abusive defensiveness which she would call 'strong' behavior.

It's what Alyssa would have done.

"Pick a boyfriend," I told her.

"I *beg* your pardon?"

"I thought you indicated that you are attracted to males and have had relationships with men. Is that correct or have I made a mistake?"

Ilsa considered the alternative and said, "No, you have not made a mistake. I'm heterosexual."

"Okay. I'm glad we straightened that out," I said playfully. "So, please, just let go of your thoughts for a moment and let the memory of a boyfriend – any boyfriend – come to mind. When you have that, please let me know."

I was being careful to be respectful. I had already gotten the gist of how Ilsa would behave if she felt *dis*-respected.

"Okay," she said. "I have one."

"Okay, good. Thank you. Now – please – tell me something about him – anything you like – anything you feel comfortable in sharing."

She scowled at me as if I were playing a trick on her and was about to betray her in some way.

"Is the memory *that* bad?" I asked facetiously. I wanted her to be comfortable; I wanted her to feel that she could trust me. I wanted to lighten the mood. "Say only what you are comfortable with," I suggested. "I mean – can you tell me his first name? Or give me some 'identifying information'? Like 'shoe salesman'?"

Something in Ilsa's manner alerted me. Or maybe it was my *reaction* to her manner that had surfaced. It occurred to me that she may have been sexually assaulted – she was, after all, an attractive woman who exuded an air of sensuality. And some studies have suggested that perhaps eighty per cent of *all* women have been molested. (If true, I wondered how *any* couple was able to have a healthy relationship.) But I hadn't noticed any obvious behavioral cues up to that point. And – other pieces of the puzzle – she had selected a male to do her 'counseling' with which may or may not have indicated anything at all: maybe she wanted a male counselor to spar with. Which wouldn't have been a bad decision if she was looking for a 'corrective relationship with a male'. Fortunately for me, I didn't have to figure any of that out: she started to talk.

"Matt," she said. "I remember a man I dated about five years ago."

'A man'? Not 'a boyfriend'? 'Dated'? Not 'had a relationship with'? 'Five years ago'? Cold words. Distancing and protective vocabulary. Why wasn't she telling me about Mister 'Recently'?

"What was Matt like?" I asked, almost not wanting to know.

"Hmm... Professional, of course. Engineer for Aerospace. Always thinking."

"What was it like being in relationship with Matt?" I *thought* I was trying to ease her into a more visceral memory, but something was beginning to send me alarm signals – just little ones - like annoying spit balls striking the back of my head.

"It was not like much of anything," Ilsa said. "We attended theatre, had nice dinners in good restaurants and talked about our work, the country, politics, and things like that."

Cold, distant words to describe a cold and distant relationship. I suspected Ilsa selected this example because it felt safe for her to reveal. "Did Matt try to control you?" I asked.

She thought that over. "No. He was a nice guy. A gentleman."

In other words, he was harmless and, therefore, boring, I'd bet. And probably no good to her since he wouldn't engage in the conflict that she had to have in order to support her theory that 'all men are controlling'.

"What happened to Matt?" I asked her. "Why did you stop seeing him?"

"I don't know, exactly," she told me. "He asked me to go away with him for a weekend. A quick cruse down to Mexico and back. I told him 'no'. After that, he didn't call me again."

"Why did you tell him 'no'? Didn't you like him?"

"He was all right," she said thoughtfully.

"Why didn't you go with him?"

"I don't know" she mused. "I didn't want to have to sleep with him."

Hmm... She hadn't been sexual with that 'safe' boyfriend but she gave off an air of sexuality. What did *that* suggest? That she could only be sexual with controlling males? I remembered one of my first impressions about Ilsa: use and discard. Did *that* mean she would only be sexual with strangers? Men who would not interfere with the way she conducted her life?

I exhaled some of the tension I had been holding and nodded in agreement with her decision to let Matt go. I had a strong feeling that he wasn't the right relationship for her. My guess was he wanted a woman, a partner, a lover. And Ilsa didn't fit the bill. But at least she was talking; she was opening up. And I *thought* I wanted to keep her engaged in remembering what her relationships – thus far – had been like. I *thought* I wanted her to evaluate her past choices.

But just then a funny thing happened to me: I realized what the tension was that I had been trying to ignore. I realized that I *didn't* want to hear about any relationships Ilsa might have had in her life. I *didn't* want to know about her lovers or her sexual experiences. I immediately recognized that it was due to my countertransference issues: in *my* mind I was equating Ilsa to Alyssa and resisting the anxiety that was bringing up. I had heard many stories of sex and abuse from female clients and I didn't want to hear what Ilsa might eventually need to say. I didn't even want to *anticipate* it! I knew they were my issues and I knew I would have to work on them - *sometime* - but that would have to wait. Right then all I wanted to do was to direct that conversation onto something 'safe'. Safe for *me*! I *didn't* want to hear about her lovers. I didn't want to hear about abuse.

Ilsa – Alyssa!

Ilsa – Alys…

Somehow I was confusing the two! And my confusion was handing me images I thought I'd dealt with. But it seemed that I had only repressed them.

Images of Alyssa and…other…

Whenever Alyssa wanted to hurt me, she would tell me stories of previous lovers – in detail. People, places, things…and activities!

I would beg her to stop! She seemed to have no idea of how much she was hurting me. But maybe she did. Maybe she was deliberately using those stories to drive me away. When she was enraged, that's how she fought arguments. She took a savage delight in winning.

The jealousy ate me alive.

I tried to focus on Ilsa across the table, but I was losing the battle. I wasn't focused on *her* needs; I was focused on *mine*!

I didn't *want* to hear about her lovers. I didn't *want* to hear about abuse. And if I had thought my legs would have carried me, I would have stood up and *left*!

She said, "I really don't have *that* much to say about relationships. They've all been rather …ordinary. Boring, actually."

Ilsa – Alyssa!

In my emotional confusion, I blurted out, "Oh, please! You know what I understand about you so far?"

"Oh, please!" she said, mockingly. "We *must* hear whatever *you* understand!"

"You came from an emotionally starved family," I told her. "And you have replicated that starvation in all your relationships. You probably smothered your first boyfriend with your neediness and tried to get from him what you didn't get from your parents. Somewhere along the way you pushed too hard. He rejected you and you've been mad at men ever since. So you take it out on *all* men by selecting inappropriate partners that you can't *possibly* succeed with. Then you re-enact that same cycle over and over again – driving people away – especially men – so that you can feel 'safe' by never having a real, healthy relationship with anybody!"

Ilsa was obviously surprised by my effrontery. People just didn't *talk* to her like that. Certainly not employees! "...ex*cuse* me...?"

But I wasn't done. Apparently I was just warming up.

"With the way you parade around the pier? The provocative way you dress? The way you flirt with men? Your air of carnal superiority? *Nobody* learns all *that* without a *lot* of experience! You *must* have screwed around with a *hundred* guys! Led them on! Used them up! Spit them out! And been screwed over *by* them! That's the usual story! The usual promiscuous merry-go-round of a lifestyle!"

I took a breath and noticed that she was listening with a bemused smile. For some reason I didn't understand and couldn't control, I kept talking.

"Now that you're completely jaded and burned out on the games you play, you start crying that *nobody cares* about you! And that your relationships are 'ordinary – *bor*ing, actually'. But *you're* the one who can't feel anything! *You're* the one who's cold and controlling! You brought on your*self* whatever bad experiences you've had! That's probably why you…why you're…"

That's when my ears finally caught up to my mouth and I heard what I was saying. I stopped dead…cold…

What was happening to me?

Abruptly, Ilsa sat up straight. Not quite offended. More like - vindicated.

I cowered – waited – and wondered: 'Where had *that* come from?' But Ilsa didn't give me time to wallow in my confusion.

"*Now* I know what you're looking for," she accused me. "You want to know what awful experience I had that has 'ruined forever' my ability to have a good relationship with a man."

Oh, no! What had I done? No, I really didn't want to know.

"*You* want me to tell you about *what*? The *first* time I was raped? And *you* want to blame *me* for that?"

No! No, actually, I didn't. I didn't want to hear the details I suspected were coming. I knew *she* needed to say it – to tell her story to *some*one. Maybe not then; not there; certainly not to me but...

Ilsa gulped some wine, almost broke the glass slamming it down, and told me: "*You* want me to confess that my first experience with sex –

my first *attack* – wasn't all that *good*? Wasn't all that much *fun*? And that's why *I* drove *him* away?"

Oh, Sweet Jesus. Please save me. The *very* thing I *didn't* want I had brought on!

"*You* want to hear the perverted details that will titillate your little weenie and – what? – sell books? Are *you* writing some little sex-po-se about the rich and famous that will make *your* name in the psychological community?"

Yes. No. That is… *You* called *me*! And I…

"Some little 'Harrod Experiment' that will make *you* famous and make the rest of us look ridiculous?"

Clearly, we had… I had…

"Well, *here's* something for your tabloid! You want to hear about Glennie? My *first lover*?" Ilsa tossed off her Mondovi like she was tossing a grenade. I waited for the explosion. Maybe this was *what* she needed to do but it was not *how* she needed to do it. And certainly not *where* she needed to do it.

"Glennie was my high school sweetheart! He was an all-around American jock. But that was the problem – he was a *guy*! Male! Man! Testosterone! And all he wanted – *needed* – to do was to *fuck* something! And *brag* about it!"

Where had I heard a story like that before? Or, rather, how many *times* had I heard it?

Ilsa dumped more wine from the carafe into her goblet – much better to quaff you with, my dear – and inhaled it before I could get a word in edge-wise. Once again, we weren't in Kansas any-more and I had stepped on a...

"He told me he *loved* me! Stop me if *you*'ve said this before! To some one of *your* bimbos! He told me that we were going to 'spend our lives together!'" Again, she slopped wine into her glass and over the table; it spread through the fine linen like a blood stain on a bridal bed. She poured it down her throat like a dead woman gasping for air. "He said it would 'be all right'. Nobody would know and we would 'be together forever'."

Part of that was true. But Ilsa was in no mood to hear it.

She dumped more of the expensive vintage down her throat. "I told him, 'No!', but he wouldn't stop!" she roared.

Other patrons were turning; watching. *I was emotionally destroyed* – not wanting to know what I already knew - what was coming.

"I was *fif*teen! We were 'out on a *date*'! Some date! He took me 'parking'! When I told him I wasn't going to fuck him, he pulled me out of the car, threw me in some bushes, held me down and pulled my clothes off!"

Oh, I didn't need to hear this but I should have been listening. I should have respectfully reflected her feelings and let her know that I *understood* her. That's the job! *That's* why I get the big...

"He pulled my skirt up and my panties down! In the *dirt*! On the *ground*! The damn bastard didn't give a shit about *me*! It was all about *him*! *Him*! He was in me, pounding like an *animal*! And off me just as fast! A *dog* would have done better! A *dog* would have at least sniffed around for a minute! But, *no*! *Glennie* was now a *man*! A *stud*! And he had to brag about it all over school! *Brag* about it!"

I felt sorry for Ilsa. I knew what she was talking about; I knew how it was. But that could never take away the pain – the lasting effects of what had been done to her. I wanted to help her – to *heal* the humiliation that was locked in her past. But to do that would require alliance – and trust. We didn't have either.

"*He* was a stud! And *I* became the Whore of Babylon! It was all over school by Monday! I couldn't face anybody! I couldn't deny it to my friends and I couldn't explain it to anybody else! I couldn't go to my proms – either one of them! And I couldn't explain *why* to my parents!"

I didn't want to hear any more. I couldn't stand another word of it.

"Now do you want to hear about the *second* time I was raped? Or the *third*?"

No. No, I didn't.

She poured even more wine down her throat to drown the pain but it did no good. Nothing had done any good since that day.

"And *you* want to know about my *relationships*? Have I explained enough? Or do you need more details?"

No. I didn't want more... I was feeling her shame. I was...

"Men are *pigs*!" she shouted. "*All* of them! They don't know the difference between a pussy and a porcupine! All they do is take! *Take*! And *you* want *me* to learn how to get along with *them*?" She emptied the last of the wine down her angry throat and swallowed it like...I don't want to say. Portions of it sloshed out of the corners of her mouth as she was unable to contain it all.

At that point, Ilsa stood abruptly up – knocking her chair backward and onto the floor. Patrons turned and stared at us. She glared at me for a moment longer – accusing eyes that held all men accountable for the sins of Adam – as though *he* was responsible for her rejection from Paradise and for everything that had happened to her because of it. *He* should have known how to care for Eve. *He* should have fixed the problem and kept them in the Garden for eternity. Wasn't that *his* responsibility? Didn't he cherish woman enough to care for her? To make certain that no evil befell her?

The glare in her eyes – the hatred: I was a 'Glennie'. I was one of *them* – the enemy, the despoilers. I understood why Ilsa was in pain. I accepted my part – the part that many men played in the anger of many women. I have never attacked *anybody* but I had failed in my obligation to protect and to love. To cherish – to hold – to cling to no other till death do us part.

In that moment *I* was the serpent in the garden. *I* was the physical representation of evil. But how could I 'fix' any of it? I was helpless before Alyssa's wrath.

Ilsa's!

No, I couldn't fix it. I couldn't fix any of it. But I was a member who knew he was tainted by his own actions and the actions of his fellow men.

"I think I'm through with therapy, doctor," she told me. "Thanks for the thrill!"

For a long, terrible moment, she held my defenseless gaze with her glare. Then finally – mercifully – she turned and stormed out of the restaurant.

When Ilsa had been gone a few minutes and the waiters had returned to their work, the other diners had stopped staring at me and I had come out of my shock, I realized that she had left me with the check.

And I don't eat Quiche.

***

After that day, I thought a good deal about my one meeting with Ilsa. She had exposed a pain in me I could not repair. And I certainly hadn't done her any good, either.

I had reenacted my failure with Alyssa in my attempt to communicate with Ilsa. I had let my unresolved emotional baggage play out with a client.

How?

I thought I had faced and resolved my personal issues, at least to the point that they wouldn't interfere with my professional work. I thought I had been better trained; I knew better; I had the experience. How and why had it happened?

I had been taught to not 'take on' the negative feelings of my clients. And I hadn't taken on Ilsa's; the negative feelings were my own, not hers. What had happened was that her behavior triggered in me a reaction – and a pain – from my past. After meeting Ilsa I did not believe I could 'see' any more clients – even if they 'tracked me down'. I did not believe I would be able to help them. What I needed to do was what I had already begun: a self-search to rid myself of the 'ghosts' that had continued to haunt me – to cleanse myself of the demons that clouded my thinking and destroyed my clarity. I needed to be rid of my own 'issues' before I would be able to help anybody else with theirs. When Ilsa left me – exposed, ashamed and humiliated in a restaurant too expensive for my budget – I knew I needed to complete what time had interrupted: I needed to return to my own counseling and 'do my own work.'

I was never able to return to Austin's – I was certain the waiters would remember me as the 'one' who had annoyed the pretty lady on a perfect summer afternoon. Besides – I couldn't afford the place.

No.

Instead I walked the pier – as I have done all the years of my life – trying to sort out my own problems and to understand the nature of men - men who had known the garden and who had abused it.

Finis

*

Bonus Section from

The Wounded Healer

"Judging from all the stories you've told me, it seems you want to complain about your job."

"Yeah... I guess so..."

"So, let me ask you. Are you a 'rescuer'? What kind of psychotherapy do you practice?"

"Humanistic, client-centered, Rogerian... Psycho-antisocial, pseudo dynamic...psycho-neuro-pathetic. The usual."

"And...uh...this 'creative' approach didn't work with that last client?"

"...I sort of lost it..."

"How did you 'lose it'?"

"Uh... I let my personal feelings get involved with my work."

"Tell me about that."

"Well, it's…hard to explain. One minute I was doing fine and the next she was screaming at me."

"It sounds like *she* 'lost it.' Why do you think *you* did something wrong?"

"Uh… I said the wrong thing. She wasn't ready. I offended her."

"Was it intentional? Or did you stumble on one of her triggers?"

"Both, I'm sure. We were in a restaurant …Austin's over here on the pier. I'm sure you know it."

"Hmm. Yes, I know it."

"And this woman just attacked me – verbally. I was unable to work her through it."

"Why couldn't you work through it?"

"…uh… 'Cause she stood up, loudly denigrated all men and stormed out of the place before I could get my foot out of my mouth."

"Do you think that she needed to get it out? To say what she said?"

"Yes, I do. But that wasn't the right time or place to say it."

"We'll get back to that. What do you think you said that was wrong?"

"Uh... Basically I told her that she was re-enacting her family of origin emotional rejection in her unsuccessful relationships with men."

"Had you known her long?"

"First meeting."

"Then why on earth did you make that interpretation?"

"Based on what she had told me, her emotional cut-off from her parents, her lack of successful personal relationship, her dismissive treatment of me and the waiters, and her self-disclosed absence of trust in her employees and other cues."

"At the time did you feel your interpretation was accurate?"

"Yes."

"And now on reflection what do you think about the exchange?"

"Hmmm… I think the interpretation was accurate but the presentation was a mite faulty."

"What was faulty about the presentation?"

"I used a Phase Two interpretation when I should have been building a Phase One connection with the client."

"To say the least. Instead of 'making an interpretation', why didn't you just back up, reframe and re-connect with your client?"

"I'm not sure. I didn't think of it at the time."

"Why not?"

"By then she was screaming at me. I was fumbling over my words. People were gawking. You know – the usual public restaurant humiliation type of counseling blunder that we've all had."

"I see. Let me ask you this. Was your 'interpretation' judgmental?"

"…'judgmental?'… What do you mean?"

"Were you trying to make her feel bad about herself? Trying to make her feel 'wrong'?"

"Hmm…maybe so… How would I know I was doing that?"

"How would you...? Let's put it another way. How do you feel about your clients?"

"How do I *feel* about my clients? Now, what does *that* mean?"

"I mean, do you like your clients? Do you not like them? Do they annoy you? Do you resent them? Have you grown tired of the work? Are they just paychecks?"

"That's an awful lot of negative choices, doctor!"

"All right. Do you *love* your clients? Do you look forward to seeing them? Are you fascinated by the work?"

"Ha! No. No. But, ah...they're definitely not pay checks. Hmm... I think...on some level...I resent them. ...yes... I think that's ...that's got something to do with how I feel."

"Why do you resent them?"

"Well... You know... They impose on you. Beyond what they have a right to. They demand extra time and attention. And emotional energy. Then a lot of them don't give anything back."

"Give anything back? Professional services are exchanged for professional fees. What *else* would you want them to 'give back'?"

"Aaah, well... I think we'd better leave *that* subject alone."

"What subject?"

"...the subject of fees..."

"All right. For the moment. Then tell me more about how they impose on you."

"You know, that's funny. Lately they just show up and expect me to drop everything and be there waiting for them. Why do you suppose they do that? Do I have the word 'sucker' painted on my forehead?"

"Do you hold appropriate boundaries with that kind of behavior?"

"No. I guess I don't."

"Maybe that's why they do it."

"...yeah...maybe..."

"You said something about 'giving back'. Some of them do? Give something back?"

"Yeah. I have to admit...some of them do."

"What do they give back?"

"Uhm... Human connection, I think. I guess that's the best way to describe it. Some of them connect with whatever is bothering them and then they open up... They get it. They learn something about themselves and they improve. That's a fascinating change to watch. And it's a privilege to be a part of it. For me, that's 'giving back.' It means my work was successful."

"Human connection?"

"Huh?"

"You said, 'human connection.' For you counseling is human connection? Don't you have a social life?"

"...yeah. Sure I do..."

"Tell me about your social life."

"All right. So I *don't* have much of a social life. ...Thanks, doc. Keep rubbing it in."

"I wasn't trying to. Okay, then. How is it a privilege to work with your clients?"

"You're in the counseling profession. You should know what I mean."

"I want to hear *you* say it. I want to know how *you* experience it."

"Uh... It's hard to describe. When a person opens up, they are vulnerable. That means they trust you, trust that you won't hurt them. Not that they think it's not going to be painful but...they trust that it's going to benefit them eventually. When they open up, you get to see the real person behind all of their defenses. And that's always beautiful. You...or at least I...can't help but be attracted to a real person. It's what I've tried to teach all my clients – that when they open up and become honest with the other people in their lives, relationships improve. People understand each other. They like each other better. Most people are afraid that their honesty will make them vulnerable – open to attack. That's why they stay defended."

"If they are honest and open up, *are* they more vulnerable?"

"Sometimes, yes. But anyone who uses your honesty against you has revealed *their* personal shortcomings, not yours. It's not that you have to stop being honest. It's just that...you know what kind of person the other person is so you know how to deal with them. You know how *much* you can trust them – and to what degree. So no matter *how* a person's honesty is received, it works out for the best in the end. *That's* what I try to teach my clients. So...where were we?"

"You were telling me how you felt about your work as a counselor. And I was getting the impression that you like working with people."

"Yeah. People are fascinating. Human behavior is the most interesting phenomenon to study."

"But apparently your work in counseling has had its...what should we call it? A down side?"

"Yes. It has."

"And what is that down side?"

"Uh... People blame you for decisions *they've* made. You're just trying to help and they...fight like hell over therapy things."

"What kind of therapy things?"

"Uhm… The defenses you point out. And the dysfunctional behavior you accurately identify. If they're not open and ready to explore their own contributions to their problems, they hate that and they deny everything."

"Like the lady at Austin's."

"Yeah… Like that. Dealing with client anger is really what counselors get paid for. The rest is fun – it's interesting! But their anger…gets difficult to take…at times…"

"You don't enjoy your clients' anger."

"No."

"It's not fun. It's not interesting."

"…no…"

"It hurts."

Silence.

"…yeah…"

*

End of this sample.

Enjoyed the preview?

The Wounded Healer is available for purchase from Amazon.com, CreateSpace.com, and other retail outlets, including the publisher: GBSPublishing.com.

Counselor's Couch

This and other titles in the series are available at Amazon.com, Createspace.com, Kindle and many other retail outlets.

Counselor's Couch: Babushka

Counselor's Couch: Gazzara

Counselor's Couch: Lolita

Counselor's Couch: Oscar

Counselor's Couch: Battle of Old Town Hill

Counselor's Couch: Gantry

Counselor's Couch: Maleficent

Counselor's Couch: Book of Shadows

Counselor's Couch: Ilsa

Counselor's Couch: the Wounded Healer

Counselor's Couch

About the Author:

Mr. Stump is a licensed psychotherapist who lives and practices near the coast in southern California. He walks the local beaches and piers regularly but does not meet with clients there. He provides Consultations for Life Transitions via the internet and the telephone.

He particularly enjoys working with interns in order to help the next generation of psychotherapists find its way.

He can be contacted through:

jimstumpcounseling.com.

ALL PRAISE BELONGS TO GOD